One Moment
One Day
One Lesson at a Time

Cultivating Your Personal Spiritual Practice

Brianné Aelysse Ellis
Spiritual Advisor/Counselor, Metaphysician

Copyright © 2020 by Brianné Aelysse Ellis

ISBN: 978-1-7346216-0-0

Contact Information

Website: andsoitiscounseling.com

Email: bespiritualadvisor@gmail.com

Facebook: facebook.com/brianne.ellis.71

Instagram: and.so.it.iz

Dedication

"People are going to write to you from around the world about how your book helped them."
In loving memory of Elaine Michelle Taylor - Thank you for everything Mommy

Table of Contents

Preface / 1

Angels / 3

Anger / 4

Anxiety / 5

Belief / 6

Celebration / 7

Confidence / 8

Death / 10

Devil / 12

Ending / 14

Eternity / 16

Faith / 17

Finances / 18

Gifts / 20

Good / 21

Heaven / 22

Help / 23

Jesus / 24

Life / 26

Loneliness / 28

Love / 30

Menstruation / 32

Money / 34

Nature / 36

Negativity / 37

No / 38

Opposition / 39

Pain / 41

Peace / 43

Regret / 45

Religion / 46

Time / 47

Truth / 48

Wisdom / 49

Words / 51

Yes / 53

Prayer / 55

Energy Never Dies / 56

Preface

Writing a book was something that I always just knew I'd do one day. I wasn't sure, in the early stages of my writing, exactly in what direction I wanted the book to go—so I just began to jot down ideas, and I felt like the Universe was downloading information through me. This book is written and inspired by life's journeys, from my perspective.

I'm a student of spirituality and religion, I find myself like a sponge soaking up all things spiritual. I have found, through my personal studies, that so many principles, philosophies, and ideas from around the world are all so similar—but some philosophies are worded in the most perfect way, so that I could digest their concepts fully and receive the gift of understanding. Many people shy away from anything outside of their religion and traditions, and that is fine if it works—but it didn't work for me.

I grew up going to church with my family. I loved church, it was all types of fun for me as a kid, and I've always been spiritual, so being at church was never a bother. Not to mention my uncle, who was the pastor at the time, had a lot of kids, so there was always someone to talk to, sit by, and giggle with. As I grew older, switched churches and began my life as a young adult, I began to pay more attention. I was a member of the ministry team and on my way to becoming a preacher. I studied under great speakers, I saw some good church services, and I built my life around the traditions of my religion. But I experienced "Church Hurt" when real-life circumstances clashed with the ideas and image I'd been studying and following throughout my whole life up until that point. There I was, at the proverbial fork in the road, and I had to choose what to follow. I had to make a choice: would it be self, or tradition? I chose self, because my spirit craved understanding. I was thirsty for it. I wanted to know and understand God, so I searched, I read, I listened, I studied.

I graduated from the University of Metaphysics in 2015 with a bachelor's degree in Metaphysical Science, and I am currently working toward my master's. I plan to eventually complete a doctorate with a focus on Metaphysical Counseling. The more I read, the more divine understanding I have. I now listen to long, deep talks on spirituality, God, Self, and Love. I mean for hours—but I had to start somewhere. This book is my version of a start. This book isn't meant to tell you how to think, nor is it meant to assume your mode of thinking is wrong, after all, what you believe to be true is indeed true for you. This book is designed to offer ideas and concepts for people who are seeking a new level of understanding. My vision is for this book to serve as a reference book, an inspirational text, and a guide for people seeking to find a way to make this life make sense. This book is meant to pique your curiosity and encourage you to dig and search: one day, when you have gained your personal understanding, it'll be your turn to share. Your perspective may be just what someone else needs for it to all make sense. I pray that my perspective brings clarity to you.

With love, I let it be so, and so it is.

Brianné

Angels

ONE OF THE FEW topics on which most of the major religions agree is the existence of angels. While different religions find differences in their purposes, the reality of their presence is unarguable.

In 2012, when I was just beginning my spiritual journey, I was blessed to find a series of books written exclusively on this topic. The author, Doreen Virtue, explains that through communication with the angels around her she was able to acquire knowledge regarding a variety of hidden things. To me, reading that book was like achieving a kind of enlightenment—it was as if I was reading the Bible, a feeling of divine understanding. The angels taught her how to pray, they told her of their purposes, and they explained the many complexities and levels of the spiritual realms.

These books blew me away. According to Doreen, the Bible, the Torah, the Quran, and most other religious books, angels were created to assist us here on Earth. They are messengers, warriors, and protectors. Angelic existence is clearly a spiritual reality: Angels are Universal, always around, assigned to us all. Angels have purpose, and they exist specifically for that purpose. It's thought that when we pass on from this life our spirits become angelic and are then tasked with helping those left behind through their own journeys here on Earth. I find comfort in that, as we all should. This is one reason why the existence of angelic beings is something humanity has always been able to agree on.

Anger

I HEARD SOMEWHERE THAT there are only two emotions: love, which has a high frequency, and fear, which has a low frequency. I have found this to be soberingly and earth-shatteringly true.

It immediately makes me think of anger. When I was angry about my family situation, I could always follow it back to a fear, a fear that things would never change. When I was angry about other people's perceptions of me, I followed that back to a fear of loneliness. There were so many things I was angry about that I discovered led either to the same or to a different fear.

So, what now? Anger is a natural emotion, right? *Wrong*. Anger takes work and energy. It takes a ton of logical willpower to connect certain actions with feelings. Here's an example: I had a fear that I would never be understood. If someone didn't agree with my thought process, I became immediately angry, thinking through fear that this person was against me. I know, I know—crazy, right? But not so uncommon: most anger can be traced to fear. Follow your anger and see where it leads. We can blame others for our emotions, but the truth is that how we react and respond is solely up to us. He or she cheated, so you got angry … justifiable? Maybe, but your root emotion isn't anger—it's fear. Fear of loneliness, fear of not being good enough, fear of lacking.

To be angry is so draining, so lasting, and so overpowering. It takes so much energy it's ridiculous.

There is good news: anger by way of fear isn't natural, meaning you can always choose a different path. There is always love. If you find it hard to love some aspect of the situation where you may be feeling angry, you can choose to simply love yourself—and you should.

Anxiety

THE MOST UNWARRANTED, CRIPPLING feelings of uncertainty—mental and physical preparation for unknown disaster, or fear. At least that's what I've felt when experiencing anxiety. It's different for everyone. Webster's Dictionary defines anxiety as:

> *Concern or solicitude respecting some thing or event, future or uncertain ... eager desire ... uneasiness ... apprehension.*

Eager desire, yes. And fear. You very seldom feel anxious about things you don't care about. Anxiety is one of those feelings you can't relate to unless or until you experience it. Feeling anxiety is not just mind-altering, but very lonely. Recently people throughout the world have become more sensitive to those dealing with anxiety. I find that to be amazing, but I also wonder—what if we eliminated fear? Would that in turn also eliminate anxiety?

In religions the word "anxious" is used, mostly, when indicating what you shouldn't do. It's considered a bad feeling. This could be one of the reasons people who experience feelings of anxiety almost never talk about it openly. But I don't think we should only talk about how fear presents itself: we need to see fear as a root cause. Look at the above definition, which talks about desire, uncertainty, and uneasiness. Why in the world would I feel uncertain or uneasy about the things I desire? When feeling anxious, ask yourself that question—and you can go a step further, to ask: *Why would I fear the thing I desire*?

Whether you have an answer or not, by asking the question you've at least begun the work. You've put your own situation and emotions under a microscope for your own growth. Anxiety, as I said before, is crippling, uneasy, and unnatural. Remove fear from your desires and remove anxiety from your life.

Belief

The word "belief" has been given boundaries. You believe, at church or in places of worship; you believe when you need a miracle; and you also believe when you're in a fairytale. Fortunately for us, we can use the power of belief daily—not just as a last resort, but as a habit. As you're reading this you have no reason to doubt that you'll inhale, then exhale, and inhale again. You don't doubt it … you believe it, you know it, it's second nature. You learned to ride a bike as a child, so you hop on a bike and know that you can ride it. You don't doubt this to be true, you believe it. What you believe is true. The Bible says faith the size of a mustard seed can move mountains … what is faith, and what is belief? Are they different?

Whether you know it or not, your faith and beliefs are constantly moving mountains. The mountains you move are up to you. What do you believe to be true about yourself? The same way taking a breath and riding a bike are second nature, what second nature thoughts have you been believing regarding you, your family, and your overall prosperity?

Believing doesn't just happen on life-altering occasions, but you are constantly believing something to be true. Make your beliefs those of positivity and prosperity.

Celebration

WHEN I THINK OF the word "celebration" I automatically think *PARTY*! I get excited when it's time to celebrate. I'm all for a party. My kids like to party, too—we can throw a party anytime, for any reason. We party in the car, in the house, in the grocery store, we will start a song and dance with "the quickness" … we will celebrate anytime and anyplace. The other night I was in my bedroom sneaking a little junk food in peace, and the kids burst into the room to ask me if I wanted to watch a movie with them. I kindly declined, and as they were leaving Chris said to Nyla "Mommy don't want to watch the movie, she's in there having a party!" I laughed to myself. It's good to celebrate, good to party: it makes you feel good, no matter how big or small the celebration. To celebrate is to appreciate. Do you celebrate yourself? Do you celebrate others? Can you celebrate life daily? All we truly have in our possession is the current moment. So, have yourself a quick party … celebrate this moment.

Confidence

CONFIDENCE IS IMPORTANT: IT's the proof of how you view yourself. Confidence is powerful: it can turn a sheep into a lion, and vice versa. Confidence is appealing: we see the wealthy, the famous, and even the average person with confidence and we think, "If I only had this, that, or the other thing I could do this, that, or the other thing …" So, we either beat ourselves up for not having something they do, or we try to get exactly the same thing in hopes that maybe we will be perceived the way, and/or feel the same way that person does.

The funny thing I've noticed about confident people is that to them, it seems so natural, like breathing. To be honest, I'm not the most confident—but I'm working on it. I see myself being more and more confident daily. The truth of the matter is that confidence really *is* as simple as breathing. I've found that the most confident people are simply living their truth; living by their own rules. When someone is living a truth that you don't agree with you may perceive it as arrogance or a person with a cocky demeanor. On the other hand, when someone's truth aligns with your thought patterns it's simply confident. I think confidence is knowing who you are—being okay with being different. Knowing in your heart that how you feel and who you are is what separates you from the crowd. That once you embrace the "you" inside, looking out the windows we call our eyes, you will become confident. You become what you notice first about those you admire: you finally look in the mirror and see *you*, not just this body that you can't understand.

How does living your truth and confidence coincide? The phrase "living your truth" is one of those things that can easily get lost in the "cliché" pile. To break it down, from my perspective it's pure honesty. Not just to and about others, but to and about yourself first. It's easy for some people to just let anything spill out, even their feelings and thoughts concerning someone else, but they may lack the ability to self-censor, and/or analyze what they've said. But being the meanest, most outspoken person isn't the same as being the most confident person.

I've been practicing being honest with myself, I've been journaling lately. Whenever I'm feeling down, weird, or insecure, I ask myself questions and allow myself time to think and write the answers down. I try not to write the very first thing that comes to mind. The reason for that is I've grown accustomed to telling myself and others what I think sounds good. A few examples of questions from the journal are:

> How often do you cry, and why?
> What do you pray for?
> What do you like to do?
> What do you think about yourself?

Every time I write I feel a little more confident in who I am. I find that whatever I feared concerning my truth isn't so scary after all—and if I can deal with my own truth, then it doesn't really matter what others may think. The other thing I'm learning is that people really don't have expectations of you. Some of us were programmed to think others need you to feel a certain way about things, and that just isn't true. If someone needs something you can't give them, they are free to find it elsewhere. That thought is freeing; it may sound a little mean, or maybe standoffish, but it's really allowing you and that other person to be free to find what each one of you needs. There is no point in wishing yourself to be different … you are whoever you were created to be, and that won't change. Embrace that truth, learn yourself, love yourself with confidence.

Death

THIS ONE IS A hard topic. It's funny, I used to always say "I handle death well." LOL! That was until three close family members died. My uncle Junie passed in October 2015, my grandma Ellis passed October 2016, and my father passed October 2017. The old folks used to say that spirits pass in threes—I guess they were right.

The reason I thought I was so good with handling death was, my mother always told us death is a part of life, and that we don't come here to stay. Those comments are both true. But when someone passes away, the physical void they leave behind is hard to deal with. What I've noticed is that when someone dies, their faults, mishaps, wrongs, and mess ups are all forgiven, so much so that all perceived negatives are now either understood or ignored. People decide that it's no longer worth thinking about. It's no longer important. It isn't like those things didn't *happen*, but instead of dwelling on them, we make a choice to forgive and forget. Is death a universal reminder that this life here on Earth is short, limited, and shouldn't be taken for granted? At almost every funeral service I've attended, someone says "give people flowers on this side of the ground." Could the bouquet possibly have a "forgiveness" flower, an "I'm sorry" flower, an "I love you," or a "let's move past that" flower? I know one thing about death: when someone passes from this life the energy they leave behind is priceless and abundant. A spiritual person would say that certainly your loved ones are always still with you!

With that being said, the death of a loved one makes you really analyze your own mortality. You begin to put things into perspective. In Seattle I attended a church called Eastlake Community, whose founder, Ryan Meeks was diagnosed with cancer—so he took some time off. When he returned he had a clear bill of health, though he would have to continue to see a doctor regularly for check-ups and such. His return service was one of the most memorable that I ever attended. To sum it up in my own words, he basically said: love like you're going to die, because you are. He said facing his mortality was hard on many levels, being a husband and a father, but he vowed to love like it was going out of style. I heard that message and took as many notes as I possibly could, as if I was in a college lecture hall. I placed my notes on my home altar. After my father died, I placed his obituary on the altar too and saw my old notes from that service. Reading them back again was divine—a kick-start for so many things, one of them being this book.

    Death is inevitable, life is precious, love is forever.

Devil

I GREW UP IN church, and an Apostolic/Pentecostal church at that …

My uncle was the pastor. We would have testimony service, where you could stand up and express yourself. Some people would get up and tell of a victory God had won. Some people would stand and ask for prayer for a tough situation. Then there were others who would stand to tell about how the devil was on their track … I remember after a while Uncle Jack started to give rules before testimony service:

> 1. You have two minutes
> 2. Don't give the devil any glory (power)!

Number one was important because some people *love* having a mic in their hand. Number two was important because some people would always start working themselves up talking about how "the devil tried to take my life," "the devil won't leave me alone," "the devil is doing this and that."

I never asked Uncle Jack what prompted him to start opening testimony service with rule number two, but I'm pretty sure it had something to with the fact that whatever you give energy to grows.

There was a study done with two plants: one was given loving energy, and the other was given negativity. The plant given the positive energy, of course, thrived and grew big and healthy. The plant that was given negative energy didn't. Energy is power. Highlighting the negative leads to destruction but highlighting the positive cultivates prosperity.

There's a book I love to read called *The Science of the Mind*. This book was written by Ernest Holmes, published in 1926. Half of Holmes speculations are now considered realities, without question. Holmes' philosophy on duality in theology was:

> *The belief in duality has given rise in theology to the idea of a God and a devil, each*

with equal power to impose upon man a blessing or a curse, and men have worshiped a devil just as truly as they ever worshiped God. Even to-day this monstrous thought is robbing men of their birthright to happiness and a sense of security. Even to-day, and openly, men still teach that there is an evil power in the universe, that there is damnation to the souls of those who do not fall down and worship—they know not what. But the time is rapidly coming when such teachings will be thrown on the scrap heap and numbered among the delusions of a frantic mentality. It has been the habit of many religious teachers of all times to hold the crowd in awe before a mighty throne of condemnation and utter destruction, till the poor, ignorant population have rent the air with their lamentations of complete despair. This, indeed, was a good method to compel the attention with the hope of salvation through some sacred rites to be performed by those whom God had appointed. In justice to such an awful performance, we would better give to these religious teachers the benefit of the doubt and say that they themselves have believed in the atrocious teachings which they have so unhesitatingly given out.

Be this as it may, the time has now come for a clearer understanding of the true nature of the Deity, in Whom we all believe, and Whom we all seek to know and to understand. That there is a God no sane person would deny; that there could be a God of vengeance and hate, having all the characteristics of a huge man in a terrible rage, no person can well believe and keep his sanity. We will say, then, and without mincing matters in the least, that the most we had better believe about such a God is that there is no such being."

Ending

Why are endings so tough?

I immediately think of a great movie, a movie that you feel in your heart could go on and on forever. Then suddenly, without warning: *The End*. In your mind, you feel—for your personal delight—that movie should have never ended.

Devastation.

Life situations and experiences are the same. There are career paths, relationships, and so many more of life's experiences that we wish would never end. But sometimes things do. The Tao Te Ching (Verse 29) and the Bible both express that things inevitably have expiration dates. The King James Bible puts it this way:

> *To every thing there is a season, and a time to every purpose under the heaven:*
> *A time to be born, and a time to die; a time to plant, and a time to pluck up that which is planted;*
> *A time to kill, and a time to heal; a time to break down, and a time to build up;*
> *A time to weep, and a time to laugh; a time to mourn, and a time to dance;*
> *A time to cast away stones, and a time to gather stones together; a time to embrace, and a time to refrain from embracing;*
> *A time to get, and a time to lose; a time to keep, and a time to cast away;*
> *A time to rend, and a time to sew; a time to keep silence, and a time to speak;*
> *A time to love, and a time to hate; a time of war, and a time of peace."*

—Ecclesiastes 3: 1-8

The message is that things happen, things are always happening. Endings happen, they are part of life's cycles. When things end we have the tendency to think, because that thing has ended, that we will now be missing out on it. That the feeling we had while attached to this thing has also ended. In the fall, when the bright leaves are constantly falling from trees, we get so excited in reverence of their beauty, their colors, even the sound of leaves crunching under your feet when you jump into a pile of leaves. We can see the beauty in the ending of the leaves. Why is that? It's because we know that in the spring new leaves will come. We've experienced the cycle of the seasons time and time again, so we're confident. We enjoy all phases of their existence: the beginning, and the ending too. With our lives there's not the same kind of sneak peek into the future, so it's hard to trust that this ending isn't the very last.

Life as we know it is a big cycle. Things begin and things end. The leaves can't control their beginning, nor can they control their end. This applies to us as well: the cycle of the sun is governed by the same force that governs the cycles within you. As the Tao Te Ching says, "the sage puts away excessive effort, extravagance, and easy indulgence." You are the master of your own life in terms of how you react to things—as they begin, and as they end. Be the sage, and let go once the season has ended. Great movies never last forever, great times never last forever, life doesn't last forever. Thankfully, bad times, horrible situations, and sadness never last forever, either. Endings are just as good as beginnings; this is how you know you are still a part of life's cycle.

Eternity

ETERNITY DIDN'T START WHEN you were born, and it won't end when your physical body dies. Eternity is constant, and eternity is now. We couple the word eternity with "the afterlife," or God, and also when we're expressing how long we'll love someone. What we don't realize is that we are always in eternity *right now*. We are a part of eternity.

I grew up frequently being ask "where do you want to spend eternity?" When asked, everyone would say *in heaven*, or *with the Lord*. We'd also get asked "Do you want to spend eternity in hell?" In immediate fear, everyone, of course, would say *NO*! Yet as I've studied, learned, and grown, I've realized that there are many people spending the "now" portion of eternity in hell as we speak.

Webster's Dictionary defines *eternity* as:

Infinite duration, without beginning in the past or end in the future ... endless time.

Infinite is defined as:

"Unlimited or boundless, in time or space ... immeasurably or inconceivably great."

The other idea that can be described this way is God. No beginning, and no end; current. The way you are living now is "how you're spending eternity" as you know it. When the flesh dies and turns into dust, what lives on and has the ability to experience eternity? The spirit. You can decide now how you're spending eternity—this has nothing to do with possessions, accomplishments, or relationships. This has to do with the spirit within you, for this is where you will spend eternity. My advice? Make sure your spirit is cultivated and in an environment where eternity doesn't feel like hell.

Faith

BELIEVING SOMETHING TO BE true that your five senses can't verify. Trusting in your intuition, trusting in the universal power, trusting in God. The Bible says "faith as a mustard seed":

> *And Jesus said unto them, Because of your unbelief: for verily I say unto you, If ye have faith as a grain of mustard seed, ye shall say unto this mountain, Remove hence to yonder place; and it shall remove; and nothing shall be impossible unto you.*

Matthew 17:20

Faith isn't just a thought process or a way of thinking, of creating a cause and effect … but more a state of *being*: who you are, your makeup. My faith in Christ is in my makeup. I will always believe in, identify with, and love Christ—because the idea of Christ is within my heart. The Bhagavad Gita describes faith as what is in your heart, too; not just the action that one would think goes into faith, but its existence in your heart. This idea isn't limited to great or prosperous notions, but the illnesses that one may allow into the heart as well.

When the disciples asked Jesus why it didn't work when they tried to heal the man, he said "Because of your unbelief." They must have had belief in order to even *try* to heal the man right? But Jesus goes on and says this type of faith comes with fasting and prayer … communion. More than a mere belief, it must be in the depths of your heart and soul, in your makeup. Jesus says then, with faith the size of a mustard seed, you can move a mountain.

I lived in Seattle for a year; there are tons of mountains there, but the most popular is Mount Rainier. This mountain is huge and ever present: even in the fog it's there … it can be seen miles and miles away. With faith, with rooted belief within your heart … scripture says you can move that mountain. Jesus and his disciples were on a mountain, and they had an experience. But the parable of the mountain is to express that nothing is impossible.

Finances

I GREW UP POOR—I mean real poverty. When I was young, I didn't notice. Everyone on my street was the same. Nobody had much of anything. But whatever we did have, we knew how to enjoy it completely. I remember for my birthday one year, when my mom didn't have much money, she went to a corner store and bought a loaf cake. It was a small loaf of pound cake. When my mom gave it to me I could tell she was upset, sad, or embarrassed, but all I could think about was how *good* that cake was about to be.

My mother was a single parent for most of my childhood, so, needless to say, there were things we missed out on. It wasn't until I got to seventh grade that I began to realize I didn't have what other kids had. Back then there was no "No Bullying" policy. You just had to endure. I don't know if it was my age or the constant reminders at school, but it was then that finances became a thing to me. It was no longer just about the experience, but more about how the experience was *decorated*. Finances suddenly had the power to take something away from you or add to who you were as a person. The vast majority of people in the world today feel that their financial status makes or breaks who they are. Yet there are still some children in slums who have absolutely nothing and feel as though they have everything they could ask for, full of joy and confidence.

As I get older, finance conversations no longer revolve around clothes and shoes—now they're about credit scores and 401Ks. Although the subjects are different, the talking has the same effect: it can make someone feel less than, or make someone seem like more. But your finances have nothing at all to do with who you are! You can't take it with you when you're gone. Finances have nothing to do with intellect. Some people think to themselves "I should've known better," or "I am at a disadvantage." Well—finance is a skill, and skills take practice. Some are good at it, and others aren't, but this has nothing to do with their character—and we have to get to a place where finance isn't a character-defining trait. Wealthy people usually have so many people around them, all thinking "this person is doing well … they must be a great person." Not the case. And alternatively, not every person facing poverty is a good person either. Who you are has everything to do with the person you are inside, whether you happen to have so-called "great financial skills," or are just not so good at financial management.

Gifts

Gifts are unique expressions of the many attributes of God. Your gifts are how God expresses *being* through you. This is why every person has a purpose.

I make a habit of seeing the beauty in all gifts. From the person who can sing so well that the universe within you hears it, to the person at your nearest daycare who can put ten toddlers to sleep. We all have gifts, and they all have purpose—even if it's simply to spark the gift of another. God is everything: how you release the gift given to you is how you shine the light of the universe for others to see.

Finding your gift is something only *you* can do. I can, however, tell you how it *feels* to express your Universal Power, or your God-given gift. It feels like an explosion within you. It feels like meeting your destiny in that very moment. It feels like heaven.

So my advice is: try everything. My gifts are translation, intuition, empathy, and speaking—these are the things that make me feel closer to the Universe, or to God. Once I figured out how to get that feeling, I couldn't stop trying to get it again. If you're unsure whether you have a gift, try something you think you'd suck at… and go from there.

Good

GOOD IS ONE OF the many labels of judging the things you experience.

When you gain immediate pleasure from an experience, you label it as good. What is "good," though? We learn it as babies: when we do what Mommy or Daddy says, we get a "Good job!" As babies, and later as adults, we crave the feelings that come from giving or receiving things we perceive to be "good." Therefore all things are judged to see if they are good. But "good" isn't really *real*. Similar to "pretty" or "ugly," it's an unnecessary judgment. So often we live from one "Good job!" to the next. We live our lives chasing after that good feeling, from one time to the next, not realizing we are chasing things that don't really matter. They are just things that we judged to be good.

Imagine somebody dropped $100, and you found it. Judging this, someone might say "Good for you, right?" As for the person who lost it, this would be "Bad for them." But in reality, it's neither; it's simply something that happened to both of you. There's an age-old question: why do good things happen to bad people? Well, the answer is that they don't. *Things* happen to *people*. You've judged some of them as good, where someone else may not have, and even if they did judge it to be good, it would still be just something that *happened*. It's easier to let so-called "bad things" go once you realize that all things and situations come on their own terms. Refuse to judge them, learn the lessons they have to offer, and you will understand the purpose. The lessons are the purpose.

Don't judge the lesson; just learn from it. The Universe is the ultimate professor.

Heaven

THERE'S A SONG I heard while visiting a church one Sunday in Boise, Idaho. The words said, "Your presence is heaven to me." I felt like my head exploded and purple smoke erupted out, like the series of commercials on TV! All these things began to flow through my mind, like a revelation. At that moment I realized that I'd been thinking of heaven all wrong.

We read about it in the Bible and hear many great things about the place where you go after death. This place has everything your heart could desire. There's no lack, no famine, no death ... It's just waiting for us, like a vacation resort. But at that moment in the church, when my mind journeyed, I thought of the people who are already living this way, right now—what would be different for them in heaven? The difference is that in heaven you are with God. What is the gift of heaven, if it's not just luxury and lack of worry? It's the presence of God.

If God's presence is heaven to me, can I experience heaven now? Or am I waiting on those golden-paved roads? Let me tell you: I can indeed experience heaven now. As a matter of fact, the Bible says heaven is inside you:

> *Neither shall they say, Lo here! or, lo there! for, behold, the kingdom of God is within you.*

—Luke 17:21

We're taught to "live right" so that one day we'll make it to heaven. "Live right," they say, so that you'll attain the ultimate prize. But God and all power are already within you—his kingdom is *within you*! We already can experience the euphoric delight of heaven, because heaven isn't about the bling: it's about the presence of God.

Help

Like many others in the world, I hate asking for help. It makes me feel incompetent, or weak—and weakness is a sore spot for me, because when I was a child showing any kind of weakness was frowned upon. Back then I didn't know why people acted like this, but I understand now why weakness was treated as such a bad thing: when you're growing up in poverty, your weakness can quickly (and will surely) be used against you. Being weak in the hood was a no-no. If you were weak in any way, you'd better learn to strengthen your pretending skills. So I learned, and I carried those same lessons into my adult life.

Not showing weakness has gotten me a long way in my career, and in parenting, and when it comes to surviving in tough situations—but in terms of emotional and spiritual growth, it's been a block. We see weakness and asking for help in the wrong way. We think that *seeming* to have it all together is the same as actually *having* it all together. But in the mind of God it doesn't work that way. We are spirit within human form: What we appear to be isn't real to begin with, and what's real never passes away. So, with that being said, what's the harm in asking for a little help?

I know some may say "I'm the helper, so who can *I* ask for help?" Well, as for me, when I'm in need of help I ask it from God. "Help" is really a term of surrender, and I find that asking for help in surrender to God puts this life back into the proper perspective. We think we're in control, but we aren't—God is. When I surrender by asking God for help, I'm saying "God, I can't do this alone. I wouldn't even try. Please give me peace in my mind as I await your instruction for the next move I should make. God, help me to let go and dwell in peace with you. For I know that your plan for my life will be fulfilled, and all that is is divine."

Once you've asked for help from God yourself, it's easier to accept help from those who acknowledge the God within themselves.

Jesus

I'VE ALWAYS HAD A special affinity for Jesus Christ. I mean, why wouldn't I? He's the heart of my foundation.

I grew up in church, a good Apostolic church where Jesus was King. In Church everything is about Jesus … it's almost like a competition, unfortunately. I viewed it as if there were levels of relationship with Jesus. The Mothers of the church held a higher rank in their relationships with Jesus, because everyone knew that the Mothers were more than likely living a "better Christian life" than everyone else, even the Pastor. The Pastor ranked after the Mothers, and so on. As kids we'd play games about who Jesus loved more—but as I grew up and began to experience life, I started to question the validity of the black church's teachings and traditions. In this process I never felt that I had to question the validity of Christ: I am a student of religion and spirituality, and most religions speak of Christ or similar beings.

Christ, known as the son of God, appeared as a being—just like you and I—possessing the power of God, walking the earth with dominion, understanding, and wholeness at a young age. Christ, being God manifested in human form on this earth, had liberty to go against what the norm was; he had the creative ability to see past traditions in new light. Christ stood in eternity, present in every moment, channeling all power. He was a rebel, as the stories have it. He didn't need permission to fulfill his destiny: let hate come, let the lashes come, let death come. Christ had a mission, and so it came to pass. The story of Christ reaches far and wide, and has been shared for hundreds of years.

I started out by saying that I have a special place in my heart for Jesus. Growing up in the black church we were told not to question God. This phrase encompassed a lot of traditions supposedly kept in God's name. Like Christ, I was never comfortable with some traditions, and I found myself one day on my knees after crying about a horrible situation. I'd just separated from my husband at the time and I felt that the whole church had decided they were on his side. Until this point the Church and its members had been my identity. So there I was, hysterically crying, so confused—and there was Christ. I felt like I was in a meditative state. I can't say if this was the first time we met in the Garden, but I can say that I couldn't remember meeting him there before that time. And this moment was pivotal for me. In that instant, questioning all that I knew, all I could relate to was that Jesus was there with me, in a garden, a forest, sitting on a log. This changed my life; I was never the same. There's a passage of scripture I reference a lot:

> *1 If there be therefore any consolation in Christ, if any comfort of love, if any fellowship of the Spirit, if any bowels and mercies,*
> *2 Fulfil ye my joy, that ye be likeminded, having the same love, being of one accord, of one mind.*
> *3 Let nothing be done through strife or vainglory; but in lowliness of mind let each esteem other better than themselves.*
> *4 Look not every man on his own things, but every man also on the things of others.*
> *5 Let this mind be in you, which was also in Christ Jesus:*
> *6 Who, being in the form of God, thought it not robbery to be equal with God:*
> *7 But made himself of no reputation, and took upon him the form of a servant, and was made in the likeness of men:*
> *8 And being found in fashion as a man, he humbled himself, and became obedient unto death, even the death of the cross.*
>
> —Philippians 2

When I think about the mind of Christ I think about the way it was so universal, yet all the while so personal, like the God.

Life

"The union of the soul and body; also, the duration of their union."

—Webster's Dictionary

LIFE IS ONE OF those words that different people interpret and understand differently. Life is dynamic, meaning there is constant change or activity. When we think of life, we think of its past and its future. But the reality is that the fullness of life is always in the present moment. I read somewhere that the past doesn't exist, nor does the future.

I used to have a bad habit of attempting to predict life's direction, thinking I was intuitive enough to foresee life's next step. Sometimes I was able to; other times I was caught off guard. This habit was the most tiring thing I ever experienced, and it went on for years. I picked it up as a child going through situations that were out of my control, yet affected me. Attempting to foresee what was next gave me a false sense of security. It made me feel like I was in control, it made me feel prepared, it made me feel like I was in front of life … but I was driving myself crazy. I was going through life as if I was watching a movie on fast forward. I was missing things that were important for my understanding. Too often we think of the "game of life" as something we have to beat—and this is wrong. Our souls decide to participate in life to expand universal understanding: everything we do, see, and experience has its purpose. All things work together like pieces of a puzzle—and in completing a puzzle there's no winner, it's not a race. Life is meant to be understood.

I no longer try to win at the game of life. I take my time now. I try to remain present for every moment. I try to silence my mind, so that I don't miss any important lessons. Life is a process: there's no manual or "how to" booklet specifically created to show you what to do next. Fortunately, within each of us there is a Guide. God within you, be the silent partner in life. God a constant help. Life can be considered hard, if you decide to view it that way;

life can be amazing if you decide to be present in every moment, quiet your thoughts, and lean on your Guide.

Loneliness

I USED TO FEAR loneliness, as if it was the worst thing that could happen to a person. Then, one day, I began to like and appreciate the company I was in when I was by myself. Now … I am willing to *pay* for alone time. It's like gold to my spirit. I have the most fun by myself, and time flies when you're having fun.

I once heard a speaker say that everyone will be lonely at some point, and that's a fact. This simple phrase spoke volumes to me. I used to view loneliness as always bad, a punishment of sorts for not being good enough. I thought if you were the perfect person, and did everything right, people would always want to be around you. But my thinking was faulty—that mindset had me out of control. I tried to reshape myself into an all-knowing, all-loving, all-doing person that could and would relate to anyone, all out of fear of being alone. I was everyone's BFF … everyone's except my own. The way I thought was sickening, sickening to myself as I look back. In reality, I was mostly just sad, damaged, and hurt. It's a bad feeling, to feel that in order to feel good you need someone else in the room. But that's where I was emotionally and mentally.

And it wore me down, because no one can scratch the itch of happiness for you, except *you*.

What I learned, eventually, was that I was done having and setting overly high expectations for people to fulfill me—so, of course, they continually failed. Because it really isn't anyone else's job to fulfill you. They *can't*. You are already full! Each and every one of us embodies a spirit. That spirit is God, the Universe, Love, the Source … the Universe is inside of you, God is within you. You are a piece of perfection, therefore you are perfect. You lack nothing. You need nothing. Yes, you came here alone, and you will die alone—but, with that being said, you have been equipped with all that you need. Once you love yourself as an expression or an extension of loving God, you gain comfort in who you are, and understanding of what the Universe has for you.

When I'm alone, my thing is either watching TV or reading. And when I do those things, I almost always find a jewel dropped by the Universe to help me in my present situation. When you connect to yourself you connect to your higher self, you connect to the Universe.

Love

I HAD A TOUGH childhood. My mother was a single parent for the most part. There were times when we had, and there were times when we had nothing. As a child I was obsessed with the idea of love, I wanted love in every way... I believed, in my heart, that if I had someone who loved me, I'd never have to worry again. Most kids in poverty dream about wealth—I dreamt of love.

As I grew older and experienced a little more of life, I started to find that the idea I had of love wasn't quite accurate. I thought love was just this *feeling* that would come over you, with the power to erase all your issues forever: happily, ever after usually ends the movie. Love has been depicted over the years as something someone else will give you, if you're lucky enough to find that person. Love is painted as some magical exclusive experience, only attainable to those who fit some made-up ideas. But these types of ideas create an unhealthy understanding of what love is.

Finally, I found that the only healthy way to quench my thirst for love was to show *myself* the love I felt I wasn't receiving. I was going through life seeking to find the person that would love my problems away. I was looking for an escape through my studies. I was looking everywhere except into *me*. But then one day I did—and I made the decision to love myself the way I wanted to be loved. This was a sobering decision: it was sobering to realize that, before that day, I hadn't been loving myself at all. I was never patient with myself. I didn't put myself first, ever. I doubted myself constantly. I was so critical of me, I even teased myself, cruelly. And I realized that this was how I was showing myself to the world. Wounded. I was hiding behind the hope that someone or something else would make everything new again, that someone or something else could change the way I viewed myself.

I'd always mentally translated the saying "God is love" to mean that God has endless love for us. That's not the case: "God is love" is literal. God *is* love, complete love. The energy that you feel when you experience love is always God-energy. When you go out of your way to help someone in need, that's showing love. When you come to the aid of a friend, that's the feeling of love. When you decide to change negative thoughts about yourself into something loving, that's God too. And love is healing.

I've found that until you start loving yourself—the being, created in the image of God, that you are—you can't give or receive the actual concept of love or of God.

Menstruation

THERE ARE SO MANY different euphemisms for when a woman is menstruating. "That time of the month." "Cycle." My favorite, "Lady days." Unfortunately, people (even unknowingly and unintentionally) view this time of the month with negativity. Women dread the day that menstruation begins, or—if they're anything like me, and they're at their current quota of children—they welcome it with the side eye. Like, "I'm glad to see you but don't overstay your welcome." The first week of menstruation for some women is a rollercoaster of emotions. When it's that time of the month for me, I experience word vomit, with no restrictions. For others it's worse: they experience *actual* vomit. As women, our bodies go under construction whether we are on board with the plans or not.

One of the hardest things I experience during the week of menstruation is that those around me can't seem to understand that I'm literally out of commission for the week. So in turn I find myself pretending to be as normal as I am any other week. This was once a spiritual hindrance for me: I got to a point where I began to dread my cycle, and dreading anything about the way you were created to be is a spiritual hindrance.

I decided to study how menstruation is handled in different cultures, metaphysical means for handling my cycle, and I hit the jackpot: I gained understanding of the purpose of menstruation. Most of what I knew of menstruation was its procreative side. What I had never learned was that this time is meant for me to quiet my mind and body, listen to my body, and relax my body. As I mentioned before, during that time of the month I'm usually letting anyone in my path have it, going off on anybody for anything. I realized that this was because I didn't feel like anyone around me respected the process happening within me. Because they didn't. How could they? I didn't either. I never openly said "Hey, this week I'm menstruating, so everyone around here will need to pull their own weight."

I was so busy dreading the feelings, the inconvenience, and the pain that I never thought to *respect* this time.

As I've begun to respect and appreciate my week of menstruation, I've learned to use it as a reminder to care for myself, to respect the changes that my body is going through. Now I listen a little more to myself during this time, and I'd encourage the men reading this to listen to the women around them during this time too: the delivery may be harsh, but the emotion is real. Menstruation is painful, time consuming, and messy—but what other time, as a woman, do you have time to take a long shower? What other time, as a woman, is it so important to sleep in? Honor this time and you'll see the results. I encourage you to research, experiment, and find your perfect treatments to make your time of the month special.

Money

WHAT IS MONEY? WHEN it's in your pocket, it's paper. When it's in the bank, it's a number on a screen. It's a form of currency.

Before the concept of money, things were exchanged using a bartering system. Then came the creation of coins. So, one day, someone sold something in exchange for a coin—or a few coins, who knows. And this person felt like the coins were of equal value to the thing they were selling. Back then, maybe they were. But now, money is a little different. I say this because you now need it for *everything*. Here in America we need money for basic survival. Whether you know it or not, we still use the bartering system too—a lot of people have bartered their lives for money, bartered their time for money, their children, and much, much more. Nothing is precious, and everything has a price, especially to those who don't have money. But really, what *is* money? Money or wealth, like everything on Earth, is energy. Have you ever been in a pinch and all of a sudden it's taken care of ... out of nowhere? The same as when you're sad and someone comes out of nowhere to cheer you up. Have you ever found money in a pocket that you know for sure wasn't there before? Well, that's also just like when you're feeling alone, and the phone rings, and it's someone who is always there for you.

Energy flows. Energy can flow *to* you, *away* from you, and *through* you. This is true of everything. When you think of money this way, it sort of diminishes the value we as humans have set for it, doesn't it? Everything in Earth is of abundance. There are people with so much wealth it's ridiculous, and they act like it's nothing, right? That's because from their perspective, it's easier to see that it's just energy. My children live a life very different from my childhood. They're privileged. They don't have to worry about money, because I don't worry about money. Money flows to me, through me, and away from me constantly. So do love, peace, and kindness. *You* are the object of worth: money is just another thing of the Earth. I know, *yeah right*, right? But think of it like this. If the president announces tomorrow that the American dollar will no longer be our form of currency, that we will now be using hairpins, how will you feel about the numbers on the screen, or the paper in your pocket? This is happening now with cyber currency. So, don't focus on currency, focus on the abundance of the Universe. The abundance of God within you.

Nature

Nature is the biggest blessing given to us by God, and a great example for how to live life. Everything on Earth as we know it came from the Source, from God. Every mountain, every valley, every ocean, and every forest. Trees grow abundantly without thought. A plant can grow through a crack in asphalt. I know plants don't have consciousness, but the example still holds. Because they aren't conscious, they don't know their purpose—but they still complete it. A tree doesn't "know" as a seed that it will one day be a thirty foot tree. It doesn't "try" to grow, it doesn't "try" to find water, it doesn't "try" anything—it simply *becomes*. That seed has no worries about the seed next to it, or the tree that's already grown ten feet taller, the seed simply receives its essentials from the source, and becomes what it is meant to become.

I think nature is a great example of how to live, because ultimately God is in control of our lives. We stress, worry, compare, do, strive, and so on… but it isn't by *our* doing that anything happens. I heard somewhere "it's not us doing, but that we are being done," meaning that we aren't really accomplishing anything by our stressing and striving and comparing, just as a tree wouldn't change its destiny by doing those things. The only thing stressing does is add more stress. Just as the seed planted will one day become a big tree, live abundantly and die, so we too will become what we are destined to be, live abundantly, and die.

Negativity

THERE ARE TIMES WHEN I find myself in this downward spiral of negativity. It's awful; I allow my thoughts to move to one negative situation after the other. It's like negativity feeds off itself.

When I get like this, I plant my feet for battle. Our thoughts determine the world around us. When we change the way we're thinking, things around us change too. It's easy to become caught up in a self-loathing state of mind, but I've learned to catch myself when I see I'm starting to go down a negative road. It's like a car rolling down a hill, picking up speed as the hill becomes steeper and steeper. Negativity consumes you and has the power to set you all the way back to where you started. This can be detrimental to all the work you've been doing to keep your thoughts clear, positive, and loving. I think everyone has negative thoughts, but I think the difference between those who can bounce back and those who can't is the willingness to do a complete 180 degree turn in your thought process. You can't allow the negativity to take over: What you think is your responsibility. It's your choice to think of the worst-case scenario.

When you find yourself wallowing in negativity:

1. Get to the bottom of the negative thoughts.
2. Change your mind, think positively.
3. Take action towards your desired outcome.

No

Many people feel bad about the word "no," but ultimately, it's the same as "yes." It's an answer to a question, it's a word, and it has letters. The only difference is in how someone reacts to the answer they hear. People don't like to say no, because people don't like to hear no. Why don't we like to hear no? We interpret it as rejection, and no one likes to be rejected. In reality this stems from the idea that we are in control of this thing called life, and the word "no" comes as a hit to our ego. And it's the same for the person delivering the no: feeling as if you have the power to hurt someone's feelings makes your ego feel as though it has more control than it really does. But the truth is we aren't in control, we can't hurt anyone's feelings. Hurt feelings are always a choice, whether they arise because you said no or because you heard it.

Opposition

"That which opposes; an obstacle … the aggregate of persons or things opposing … in politics and parliamentary practice, the party opposed to the party in power."

—Webster's Dictionary

"But I say unto you, That ye resist not evil: but whosoever shall smite thee on thy right cheek, turn to him the other also."

—Matthew 5:39

"Evil is a projection of our own shadows—the yin and yang of life; if you shine light on the shadows and forgive them you can diminish them."

—Deepak Chopra

When I was first introduced to the word opposition, it seemed to embody the idea of the "Devil's job." Opposition, as I knew it, was something that came from the devil. At least that's how I knew it then—but I learned, afterwards, that opposition isn't real when you know and believe God's will for your life will come to pass. When you believe in your destiny and purpose, no opposition can be real. Nothing can oppose God: God is everything.

I'd suggest renaming the things that seem to oppose you in your life as redirectors. The ego has a tricky way of making you think everything is about you personally. It can also make you think you're on the opposing team of life—and that isn't true. Life is your gift. Of all the living things on Earth, we are blessed with complex consciousness. We embody the potential to create: we can make something from nothing, right here on Earth. Think about how, before there were tables, there was no such thing; someone, in their mind, thought of such a thing and put their creative potential to work. Within *you* is something waiting for you to acknowledge it, to bring it to fruition. And in the midst of your creation there may be redirectors. Things happen, and sometimes things have to happen. When you're faced with opposition see it as an opportunity for redirection and push forward.

Life isn't against you; there is no opposition, only redirection.

Pain

Pain presents itself in many ways, but spiritually it can be said to come from within. Some holistic health practitioners treat pain through emotional channels. I once read a book in which the writer described how a woman came to her complaining of shoulder pain. The practitioner wrote that through body work and visualization she was able to assist the client with childhood issues that she had been carrying around for years. She'd been tense without knowing it, holding on to things she didn't know how to release. After working with the practitioner, though, she was finally able to release the pain both emotionally and physically.

Emotional pain is a doozy, because it's both tricky and unconscious. When experiencing physical pain you know your limits: you can forget about bowling with a sore shoulder, forget about skating with a sore ankle, and don't even *think* about those cute pumps with a sore toe. Physical pain stops you in your tracks and tells you *sit down, pay attention to this area and rest it*. That's where emotional pain is different … you can go way past your unconscious emotional limits without realizing it until it's too late. I've made it to the middle of so many bridges and looked back only to find the bridge broken behind me—missing planks and really raggedy. I use this metaphor because sometimes, in life, we go further than we're emotionally ready to go.

There have been several tear-filled instances in my life when I looked back at myself and had to say *I didn't know there was so much pain there, but now the bridge is broken and there's no going back*. At that point you can either sit there, or you can press forward. Pressing forward with emotional pain is very similar to healing physical pain, meaning, you pay attention to the place where you are hurting.

There was a period in my life where I was totally unhappy. I was miserable, and in a lot of emotional pain. I felt incomplete, drained, and afraid. I was in the middle of a really big bridge in my life: I had walked out on my own and there was no one there for me to call. I could scream if I wanted, but nobody would hear me. So, I metaphorically sat down in the middle of that bridge, and I stopped moving forward. Fear and emotional pain had crippled me, my ego kept trying to make me believe I could fix whatever was wrong, but I couldn't—this pain was far beyond my control. And I was not able to heal until later, when, in my reading and my listening, God spoke to me, letting me know that the same universal, creative, strong, mighty force at work outside of me resides also inside of me. That I am a part of the whole, I am a figment in the mind of God. I realized then that if I continued to think *I can*, or *I can't*, or that I was in control of my past, my emotional pain would swallow me whole. I had to surrender my will, thoughts, and desires to God the healer, the way maker, the I AM. See, I had allowed myself to believe it was due to my own merit or smarts that I had made it to the midpoint of that bridge, and that was why looking back at its remnants was so scary. I could only overcome that fear once I realized it's not about me, the bridge, or the destination; it's about the power and the presence of the Source.

    Emotional pain is tricky because it lives in your unconscious mind … but it's only real there. In the reality where God dwells, there is no pain: God is perfect peace.

Peace

My knowledge about peace can be compared to the tip of an iceberg: most of it is unknown and unseen.

Growing up I thought peace was either a prize or a gift that really good and holy people can have, or something I would obtain with age. I grew up watching my grandmother, who seemed so unbothered all the time, it felt like nothing could surprise or upset her. I grew up in church hearing songs that repeated positive affirmations— "Joy is mine, Love is mine, Peace is mine," and so on—but in those songs there's no explanation on *how* you get peace to become yours. Since then I've come to learn that peace simply *IS*, just as God *IS*. The idea of peace as an accessory you have the ability to wear this or that day, or a gauge that determines the amount of peace available to you on this or that day … I learned that peace isn't that.

Peace is ever-present: peace is always peace, it never changes and never runs out. Peace is always the same, always available *to* and *for* you, and all you have to do is acknowledge it. So why is it that there are so many miserable people? Why is it that so many people feel like they're never at peace? It may be due to the fact that they don't know how easily accessible peace is. Life can mold your mindset, when you've grown in an environment where peace isn't acknowledged, to think of the idea of peace as a novelty. There are people who most would consider peaceful, judging by their finances, but in reality they can't find peace anywhere.

"Peace," among many other nouns, is one of what are called the attributes of God. God is peace, God is love, and so on. So, for example, if I told you I am rose-scented, when I stand next to you you should smell the roses. It works the same way with peace: God is peace, he is ever-present, can't leave you; you are the embodiment of his idea. So why aren't you feeling peaceful? Maybe it's because you don't realize that God is always *right here*, in every moment of eternity, emitting peace from within you. If you don't know this, or don't let yourself know, you don't get a chance to experience that peace. And that's like considering yourself poor with a backpack full of money. Without looking in the bag and finding out what's in there, you'll just continue to miss what is readily available to you at all times.

Today, I can access peace with the simple thought that peace is always here and now. I make sure I remember to acknowledge God's presence within me, which in turn reminds me that because God is within me, I must have access to all the Universal attributes of God. I can now say that in times of trouble I rely and lean on the Peace of God within me.

Regret

Regret is one of those things that, when you ask people about theirs, they always say they don't have any.

I used to say the same thing, and in a way I don't—in terms of how all my actions, choices, and decisions landed me in this place right now. But I'd be lying if I said I never wondered *what if I had done things differently*? I know, though, that to dwell in the past is a big way to remain stuck in stagnation. When you let yourself be filled with regrets your mind constantly replays something that already happened, the way it happened, and how you wish it'd happened differently. To live in regret is to live with limitations, restricted solely to the way you envisioned things going "had they gone right." And this is like saying to the universe, or to God, that the divine path of your life was all wrong. Living in regret also means telling yourself, without knowing it, *who I could've been, what I could have done, can no longer be*. Living this way, of course, breeds feelings of misery and feelings that you aren't where you think you're supposed to be.

Rewire your mind concerning the things you regret. Change what you've been calling a *negative* into a *positive*. Rework the idea that you can't be what you want. God is limitless—what you desire can still be yours. There isn't just one way to do anything. If you feel regret about a situation in the past, the best thing to do is consider the lessons you learned from the experience. Don't write it off as a total negative; some things happen, and some things never happen. That's just life.

Don't become a prisoner to things that happen in life, learn from them and move forward. That's ultimately where we're headed, anyway!

Religion

Everybody's right, or everybody's wrong. It's a good thing this section is towards the end, because my Christian friends and family will probably put the book down at this point...

Just kidding, but really, we must think of religion logically.

The idea of God is so vast there couldn't *possibly* be only one understanding of it. Between all the different religious sects, there are several different ideas. Within the Bible itself, God is called by different names. Why are there so many differences, if they are all referring to the same source? Because people are individuals, and we experience things in different ways. The world would be a very different place if people everywhere acknowledged that we're all praying to the same God—the problem is, everyone wants their idea to be the *right* one. I say all the time: Heaven will not be filled solely with Holy Ghost-filled Pentecostal believers, nor will Heaven be solely filled with Monks.

Dr. Masters, a metaphysical teacher and founder of the University of Metaphysics, speculates that the reason there are so many religions is that different people are at different stages of consciousness. For example, I consider myself a Christian, because I believe in Jesus Christ. But I often read the Hindu book called the Bhagavad Gita, and when I do, I receive the same direction and hear the same voice of God that I would If I was reading the Bible. As my consciousness of God grew throughout my journey, I began to crave other perspectives of God—I am a firm believer that the search is the point, that unless you dig and reach out, you'll stay in the same place, without growth of any sort. I'm not saying you should stop believing what you believe, or how you believe it. I'm just saying don't stop searching, either: go a little further, study a little deeper. If you aren't open to reading any other religious texts, then find study material, commentary, guides, and books related to what you believe. I'm sure you will receive a new perspective of the universal God.

Time

I USED TO SAY and believe that "time doesn't exist," until I got old enough to realize just how *real* time is. Time doesn't exist for our spiritual selves, the God part of us is timeless … but this physical life we're living is definitely on a schedule. I now believe time is one of life's most precious commodities, along with love and faith. I once heard someone say: *one thing you can't buy is time*.

When it comes to time, youth is both a blessing and a curse. When you're young, you're fearless, creative, and enthusiastic. The issue is, you think you have time to get to all that stuff later. Then *later* becomes *today*, or *yesterday*, or *last year*. We begin to say things like "time flies." I heard a comedian say time doesn't fly—it's day in and day out. But time flies when you're taking it for granted, and when you're living outside of the present, whether it be in the future or past.

There's no time like the present

Being present is the best way to respect time. When you're fully present and aware, you make use of every minute. In the present, life isn't put off until tomorrow—it's lived today.

I believe there is a reason for the way our physical bodies are on a time limit. If we didn't have the understanding that this life will end, nothing would ever get done or be accomplished. So I pray to make each present moment count. To fulfill the purpose of that moment. To meet God in that moment. To gather strength, courage, and direction in the present moment. I have to, because I'll never get that time back.

Truth

Today Chris, Nyla, and I were in the car. We were going somewhere, and I was using the navigation system. Suddenly, the guide said that it had lost the signal. Chris thought that meant we were lost, and he yelled, "Mommy, we're lost?"

I told him "No." I asked him, "Do you feel lost?"

"No," he said.

I told him that humans are smarter than computers. Then Nyla told me, sounding shocked, "Mommy, did you know Wikipedia can be wrong?" She was overwhelmed by what she perceived as trickery. So, I explained this to them (a more simplified version):

The only way to know the truth is through the divine knowledge we receive from within. We can read, study, and learn for eternity—words from other people's truths. But the only way to know the truth of anything is to know that thing.

Nyla had just completed a report on the actress and musician Raven-Symoné, and while doing her research, she had found conflicting information. Now she has learned to question all that she reads. Like the Bible tells us, "taste and see": we are instructed to find out. We're all born with a navigator within, we all have universal knowledge and universal truth within. Your truth will always be what the God in you verifies to be true—so trust your vibes, trust your core.

Wisdom

When I was a young girl people around me would say "Wow, you're so wise for your age!" But the older I get, the more I realize that I really didn't know anything back then. I'd been living a life of regurgitated ideas that wise people around me had told me. They were wise because of the things that they had gone through—this made me believe that I had to go through a lot of things, too, in order to gain wisdom.

Wisdom is a gift: it comes after you've learned from your experiences, and not always when you came out on the good end of those experiences. You can receive the gift of wisdom even after you've been beat by some of your experiences. We can easily think the wise are those who are doing well in life, but I must say, a lot of the wise things that I know came from me learning and watching those who haven't done so well in life. Even the people that would be judged by our so-called standards as "abnormal."

Wisdom is one of the most important things I seek to gain from this life. All the things I've learned throughout my years and experiences have given me a lot of wisdom, and I believe the purpose of wisdom is to share it. As a species we use wisdom to grow and evolve, so sharing what you know is mandatory. Wisdom is the medal you carry once you've come out on the other side of your trials and tribulations. Wisdom is the satchel of knowledge you have as your reward for standing through the tests that come your way.

Having wisdom doesn't necessarily mean that you don't *go through* things or that you aren't affected by life. It's the opposite: you've been through a lot, and maybe you've gone through the same things over and over and over again. Wisdom is the angle that changes. In my opinion, learning is the point of our existence on Earth—so if there are things you have gone through, or things you are going through currently, if nothing else you should know you will gain wisdom and gain greater understanding from them. Even those who have failed in the same lesson more than once are granted the opportunity to face it again, and each time they will add more pebbles of wisdom to the satchel, the invisible satchel that we carry with us.

Words

1 In the beginning was the Word, and the Word was with God, and the Word was God.
2 The same was in the beginning with God.
3 All things were made by him; and without him was not any thing made that was made.
4 In him was life; and the life was the light of men.
5 And the light shineth in darkness; and the darkness comprehended it not.
6 There was a man sent from God, whose name was John.

—John 1

WORD - λόγος, lógos, log'-os; something said (including the thought); by implication, a topic (subject of discourse), also reasoning (the mental faculty) or motive; by extension, a computation; specially, (with the article in John) the Divine Expression (i.e. Christ)

—Strong's Concordance

Word - /wərd/

noun

The spoken sign of a conception or an idea; an articulate or vocal sound, or a combination of articulate and vocal sounds, uttered by the human voice, and by custom expressing an idea or ideas … Hence, the written or printed character, or combination of characters, expressing such a term; as, the words on a page.

—Webster's Dictionary

Growing up in church I heard sermons preached from these verses over and over. They all figuratively paint a picture of a God in human form, calling forth the Earth as we know it today. They'd describe the foretelling of Christ, in an attempt to portray God's Omnipotence. God is omnipotent—but this scripture actually tells another story.

"Word," from this scripture, translates to the Greek word *lógos*, which translates to "thought," not necessarily "speech."

This means that the Earth as we know it was created by the *thought* of God.

We're familiar with the saying "words have power." But how familiar are we with the understanding that *thoughts* have power? When I was first taught about thoughts, I was told that God hears all of them… for me, this is yet another scare tactic used by people who really don't understand the power we have. The truth is, our thoughts are God; God is our thoughts.

God is thought, God is *lógos*. Not speech, but divine expression.

Our thoughts run at a faster pace than our emotions or our words. When you understand the power of your thoughts, you'll understand your power through God.

Yes

To say "yes" is to allow something. We love that word, "yes"; we've been trained since childhood to believe that "yes" is a good answer. Oftentimes we like it because it makes us feel we're gaining something; but when we feel like there's a chance we will lose something through a *yes*, then it has the same effect on us as a *no*.

Saying "yes" to a question like: "Do you want some coffee?" is different than saying *yes* to life. There can sometimes be a feeling of losing control when you just "allow" life to happen with your *yes*.

For most of my life I'd ignorantly thought that I was in control, that I was so great that I could just make it all happen. I was willing to stress myself out, cry, hurt, and so on, just to feel like I had a grasp on life; and I did have a grasp, but that was all. Life was pulling me where it wanted, like a rag doll hanging out a car door on the highway. I had always somehow thought that was the way it was supposed to feel, so I didn't realize I was being yanked and pulled until I couldn't take any more. I was exhausted. I was fighting against the current. I was basically telling life "No, *I* got this, *I* can orchestrate my plan to be better than the Universe's plan for me." I was reaching my goals, so I thought "This is my doing. I'll keep killing myself—at least people will see I died making it happen for me and my kids." That was a big misconception, and I later learned the name for that bossy, hard-headed beast inside me: the EGO.

Dr. Wayne Dyer, who my sister and I call Uncle Wayne, says the ego can be simply defined as Edging God Out. Saying *yes* to life is an action of surrender. And it isn't like throwing in the towel in defeat; I'd rather think of it in this way: the house always wins. In life we're temporary guests of this house called Earth, of this dirt called flesh, and of this galaxy we call the Milky Way. Your *yes* places you in alignment with the movement of life.

Uncle Wayne uses a metaphor of swimming with the current: it's a better flow, it's easier. I'd rather swim with the current than continue hanging onto life by a thread.

Saying *yes* to life is freeing. It allows you live blamelessly. It allows you see the divinity in others, and it changes your own perspective on who you are.

Prayer

Thank you, God. You are my refuge, my peace. I thank you: when I feel lost you are there. You never leave me. My heart longs for your presence. Your peace sustains my soul. My life I surrender to you, oh God. I continually surrender, I surrender all. When I feel unsteady you uphold me, through my willingness to surrender; I am yours. I am whole, lacking nothing. I am a divine manifestation of God. I am. I am peace, I am whole, I am love, I am whole, I am healed. God is my shelter. God is complete; therefore I am complete in God. My life is a gift from God. God's light radiates within me. In your presence, God, I am whole. Your presence sustains me. Your grace, love, and presence make me whole.

Energy Never Dies

An ode to the ones that paved the way for me who have now passed on.
Martha Ann Spencer-Williams
Urshelene Drewry
Elaine Taylor
Rodney Lynn Ellis
Richard Jones
Tyrone Spencer
Essie Ivy
Mary Spencer
Trish Spencer
Ray Lawler
Karen Lawler

AT RAY'S FUNERAL HIS body lay there in a casket, lifeless. I was confused. I thought I was there to say goodbye, but I didn't get to. He wasn't there. I couldn't cry. I didn't feel anything, until his friends began to stand up to speak. Then, it was almost as if he was standing there next to each of them. As people began to speak of his presence and his energy as it related to them, I began to feel. I realized that everyone's energy is somewhat incomprehensible until you relate it to you. That doesn't die. The energy that is created through human relationship never goes away. It just repurposes itself. We create energy by means of how we relate to one another: this is why we have friends that we consider family.

In death forgiveness is easy. We realize we will no longer have the opportunity to create the energy that made you recognize the person lying lifeless before you. All that is left is the energy from memories that once were. So as you still can, forgive now, understand now. We're blessed with a gift, that our memories can bring the energy of our loved ones forward into us. You can't change the past, but right now you can change how that energy relates to you today. In death we drop everything for a moment to revel in memories of the body that has gone on, from ash to ash, from dust to dust. We allow ourselves to drop the baggage of past hurts, insecurities, and perceived failures. I was upset with Ray the last time I talked to him, I fussed and I hurried off the phone. He was just being himself, but I thought he should've done something different. Now, in his absence, I realize that whatever he did really didn't matter. The energy of who he was to me remains the same.

    For anyone in mourning, as I am: know that what's real never dies. I see Uncle Junie in all of his children. Grandma Ellis's energy radiates through every plant and flower that I see. My father is ever present in my thoughts of freedom and choice. Martha Ann is the strength that was passed down to all of her granddaughters. Ray's energy radiates in service to others. My mother's energy continues to push me and guide me. I hear her voice and feel her presence through music and TV.

    For you, if you have lost someone—keep those memories, and keep that same energy. Energy never dies.

www.ingramcontent.com/pod-product-compliance
Lightning Source LLC
Chambersburg PA
CBHW081236080526
44587CB00022B/3961